STECK-VAUGHN

W9-AZX-524

HEADLINES OF THE CENTURY

1920-1929

Melissa Stone Billings

Henry Billings

STECK-VAUGHN
COMPANY
A Subsidiary of National Education Corporation

Books in this series:

Headlines of the Century 1910-1919

Headlines of the Century 1920-1929

Headlines of the Century 1930-1939

Headlines of the Century 1940-1949

Acknowledgments

Executive Editor
Elizabeth Strauss

Project Editor
Kelly Krake

Designer
John Harrison

Electronic Production
Shelly Knapp, Kristian Polo

Photo Editor
Margie Foster

Illustration Credits
David Griffin, p.3

Photo Credits

Cover (inset) Photograph by Harry Burton, The Metropolitan Museum of Art Pp. 5, 6 UPI/Bettmann; p.7 AP/Wide World; p.11 Culver Pictures; pp. 12, 13, 14 UPI/Bettmann; pp. 15, 19 Culver Pictures; p.20 National Baseball Library & Archive Cooperstown, N.Y.; p.21 UPI/Bettmann; p.22 National Baseball Library & Archive Cooperstown, N.Y.; pp. 23, 27 UPI/Bettmann; p.28 Culver Pictures; p.29 The Bettmann Archive; pp. 30, 31, 35, 36, 37 Culver Pictures; p.41 Photograph by Harry Burton, The Metropolitan Museum of Art; p.42 Photograph by Egyptian Expedition, The Metropolitan Museum of Art; p.43 Photograph by Harry Burton, The Metropolitan Museum of Art; p.44 (top) © Ashmolean Museum, Oxford; p.44 (bottom) Photograph by Harry Burton, The Metropolitan Museum of Art; p.49 (JF) Christianson-Leberman Studio; p.50 Culver Pictures; p.51 UPI/Bettmann; p.55 Culver Pictures; pp. 56, 57, 58 The Bettmann Archive; p.59 UPI/Bettmann; p.63 Culver Pictres; p.64 (top) Archive Photos; p.64 (bottom) Culver Pictures; p.65 Archive Pictures; pp. 69, 70 Goddard Collection/Clark University Archives; p.71 UPI/Bettmann; p.72 Goddard Collection/Clark University Archives; p.73 Culver Pictures; pp. 77, 78 © The Walt Disney Company; p.79 Archive Photos; pp. 83, 84 UPI/Bettmann; p.85 Pasadena Tournament of Roses.

To teacher: This product is reflective of its time. When necessary to the content and understanding of the story, we have chosen to use the names by which ethnic groups were known at that time.

ISBN 0-8114-3292-0

Copyright ©1994 Steck-Vaughn Company. All rights reserved. No part of the material protected by this copyright may be reproduced or utilized in any form or by any means, electronic or mechanical, including photocopying, recording, or by any information storage and retrieval system, without permission in writing from the copyright owner. Requests for permission to make copies of any part of the work should be mailed to: Copyright Permissions, Steck-Vaughn Company, P.O. Box 26015, Austin, TX 78755. Printed in the United States of America.

1 2 3 4 5 6 7 8 9 BP 98 97 96 95 94 93

Headlines of the Century 1920-1929

In 1920 American women got the right to vote. Many African Americans, called blacks or Negroes at this time, felt that the United States would never treat them fairly. Some, such as Marcus Garvey, thought about moving to Africa. The years between 1920 and 1929 are sometimes called the "Roaring Twenties." Car sales boomed. Motion pictures finally learned to talk. And many people felt a greater sense of freedom to try new things.

Contents

MARCUS GARVEY CALLS FOR AFRICAN NATION

August 3, 1920—Madison Square Garden was rocking last night. More than 20,000 blacks gathered there. They listened to music for two hours. Then Marcus Garvey rose to speak. The crowd leaped to its feet and cheered wildly for five minutes. Garvey announced, "It is time for the 400 million black people of the world to claim Africa for themselves." The crowd roared again.

Marcus Garvey in New York City in 1922

A Born Fighter

Marcus Garvey had always had fire in his eyes. Born in 1887, he grew up poor on the island of Jamaica. He was a good student. Garvey read every book he could find. At the age of 14, however, he had to leave school and go to work.

Garvey soon learned how hard life was for black workers. He began going to street meetings and discovered he was a great speaker. He became active in **politics**. He complained to the British government about **mistreatment** of blacks. When they did nothing, Garvey decided blacks could never get **justice** from whites.

On August 1, 1914, Garvey took a bold step. He set up the **Universal** Negro Improvement Association (UNIA). The purpose of UNIA was to draw "the peoples of the race together." Garvey believed black people must first learn to be proud of their race. He also thought they must own their own businesses. Finally, Garvey **demanded**, blacks must have their own nation in Africa.

Big Plans

In 1916 Marcus Garvey came to the United States. At first, no one knew who he was. But that soon changed. Garvey started his own newspaper called the *Negro World*. He traveled across the country giving **persuasive** speeches. "We demand that the white, yellow and brown races give to the black man his place in the world," he said. "We ask for nothing more than the rights of 400 million blacks."

The key was his "Back to Africa" program. He felt that blacks could never be truly free in the United States. This country was controlled by whites. Blacks had to run things for themselves. Once Garvey was told that white people might give UNIA some money. "We don't want their money," Garvey answered. "This is a black **movement**!"

Garvey's business failures caused him many problems.

Garvey spoke at Madison Square Garden.

The Death of a Dream

By 1920 Garvey's ideas had really caught hold. The UNIA had more than two million members. Garvey's movement, however, was already in deep trouble. Earlier, in 1919, he had started a shipping company called the Black Star Line. It was owned by thousands of blacks who had paid $5 a **share**. The Black Star Line was supposed to be used for trade with Africa. It was a bold dream. Garvey, however, was not good at business. By late 1921, the Black Star Line was broke.

Other businesses started by Garvey also failed. Worse, the black African nation of Liberia **rejected** him. Garvey had hoped to use Liberia as a place for his nation to begin. In time, he felt, the whole of black Africa would become **united**. But the leaders of Liberia decided they didn't want to be part of Garvey's plan.

Within a few years, the UNIA fell apart. Garvey tried, but failed, to start it again. When he died in 1940, only a few people noticed. His ideas about black pride, however, lived on. Today several African nations, as well as Jamaica, honor Marcus Garvey as a great leader.

Building Vocabulary

■ Read each sentence. Fill in the circle next to the best meaning for the word in dark print. You may use the glossary.

1. Garvey decided blacks could not get **justice** from whites.
   ○ a. jobs   ○ b. information   ○ c. fairness

2. Garvey **demanded** that blacks make their own nation.
   ○ a. forgot   ○ b. wrote a book   ○ c. asked strongly

3. His speeches were **persuasive**.
   ○ a. made people agree   ○ b. too long   ○ c. hard to hear

4. People paid five dollars a **share** for the Black Star Line.
   ○ a. family   ○ b. part of ownership in a company
   ○ c. part of a meal

5. Liberia **rejected** him.
   ○ a. turned away   ○ b. honored   ○ c. looked at

6. Garvey said, "This is a black **movement**."
   ○ a. people working together   ○ b. trip   ○ c. dance

Part B

■ Write the best word to complete each sentence. Use each word once.

mistreatment	Universal	politics	united

Marcus Garvey became active in (1)_____. He tried

to end the (2)_____ of blacks. Later, he set up the

(3)_____ Negro Improvement Association. He hoped

this would help all black people become (4)_____

Writing Your Ideas

- Imagine you are Marcus Garvey. On a separate sheet of paper, write a short speech you would give about justice for African Americans today.

Remembering What You Read

- Answer the questions.

1. What was the purpose of the Universal Negro Improvement Association? _____

   _____

2. What was *Negro World*? _____

   _____

3. What happened to the Black Star Line? _____

   _____

4. Where did Garvey hope to start his black African nation?

   _____

Thinking Critically—Conclusions

- Finish each sentence by writing the best answer.

1. Marcus Garvey left school at the age of 14 because_____

   _____

2. Garvey felt blacks could not be free in the U.S. because_____

   _____

3. Garvey did not want white people to give money to UNIA because

   _____

4. All of Garvey's businesses failed because_____

   _____

5. Today Garvey is honored in Jamaica because_____

   _____

WOMEN GET THE VOTE!

August 18, 1920—The battle is over! After years of fighting, the women of America have finally won the right to vote. Until today each state could decide for itself whether to let women have a voice. Some states let them, others did not. A change to the Constitution has been accepted today. This change gives women in every state the right to vote.

Seventy Years of Fighting

The battle over women's "**suffrage**," or voting rights, had been going on for more than 70 years. By 1918 it looked like the idea was finally **advancing**. Many felt women had earned the right to vote. After all, women had been very important during World War I. While men were off fighting, women kept the country going. They worked on farms and in factories. They took jobs in offices and hospitals. "If we can do all that," said one woman, "then surely we should be able to vote."

The U.S. **Congress** agreed. For years Congress had refused to support voting rights for women. But on June 4, 1919, it took a bold step. Congress accepted the 19th **Amendment**. This amendment stated, "The rights of citizens of the United States to vote shall not be **denied** . . . on account of **sex**."

Women marched in parades to show their support for suffrage.

A leader of the "Suffs" raises her glass of juice to toast Tennessee.

Congress wanted this statement added to the Constitution. It could only be added, however, if enough people wanted it. After Congress **approved** it, three-fourths of the states had to agree to it. Only then would it become law.

When suffrage leaders heard what Congress had done, they were very excited. "We need 36 states to approve the amendment!" they cried. "Then at last, we will have a voice in this country!"

Not everyone was so excited.

There were many who did not want women to vote. Some were factory owners. They hired women at very low pay. "Women voters would pass laws to raise workers' pay," grumbled these owners.

Other people were against suffrage because they thought it would hurt family life. How could women care for their families if they were **involved** in government and voting? "Home is the woman's world!" these people cried.

"Suffs" and "Antis"

And so the battle lines were drawn. Everyone, it seemed, became either a "Suff" (in favor of suffrage), or an "Anti" (against it). The Antis wore red roses as their sign. They pinned these roses to their jackets and dresses. Suffs pinned yellow roses to their clothes. In state after state, these two groups **squared off** to fight over the question of women's rights.

In a few states, the 19th Amendment was passed very quickly. Six states voted for it in eight days. Others followed more slowly. By February 27, 1920, 33 states had approved it. The next month West Virginia and Washington did the same. "One more state!" cried the Suffs. "Just one more state!"

The Antis counted up the states on their side. Six had voted against the amendment. Five others were sure to do the same. "That leaves Delaware and Tennessee," the Antis said. "If we win those two states, the amendment is dead."

It was true. Delaware and Tennessee held the deciding votes. On June 2, 1920, Delaware voted against the 19th Amendment. Now only Tennessee was left.

A woman's family comes to see her vote for the first time.

13

Men and women stand in line to register to vote.

Throughout the summer of 1920, Suffs and Antis poured into Tennessee. They wrote letters and held meetings. They gave speeches and put up signs. Each side tried to get Tennessee lawmakers to see things their way.

At last, on August 18, everyone gathered for the vote.

"It's going to be close," Suffs whispered to each other. "We need 49 votes to win."

"Do we have that many?" someone asked.

"Who knows?" answered another woman. "At this point, nothing is certain."

Following a Mother's Advice

Indeed, nothing was certain. Several of the 96 lawmakers had switched sides. Some had been given money to change their vote. Others had received frightening messages warning them to change their vote. A few lawmakers now refused to say how they would vote. The Suffs could count 48 lawmakers who would vote for the amendment. But would they get the extra vote they needed? As the voting began, leaders on both sides held their breath.

As it turned out, the question lay in the hands of a young man named Harry Burn. Burn was only 24 years old. He was the youngest lawmaker in the state. All summer Burn had worn a red rose on his jacket. But just before the vote took place, he had received a letter. It came from his mother. "Dear Son," it said, "Hoorah, and vote for suffrage!"

When it came time for Burn to vote, he thought of his mother's words. "I know that a mother's **advice** is always safest for her boy to follow," he later said. "And my mother wanted me to vote for the amendment." And so, to everyone's surprise, young Harry Burn stood and made the 49th vote for suffrage. The 19th Amendment to the Constitution had been approved.

The crowd went wild. Suffrage leaders threw their yellow roses into the air. They cheered and cried and sang out the news. At last all women in America had the right to vote!

After years of effort, women finally win the right to vote in 1920.

15

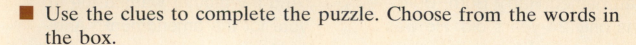

Building Vocabulary

■ Use the clues to complete the puzzle. Choose from the words in the box.

advice
involved
amendment
suffrage
sex
denied
approved
advancing
Congress
squared off

Across

1. moving forward
3. change made to a law
5. faced each other in a contest
6. male or female
7. be part of something
8. someone else's idea
9. refused to give something

Down

2. group of leaders who make laws
3. agreed to
4. the right to vote

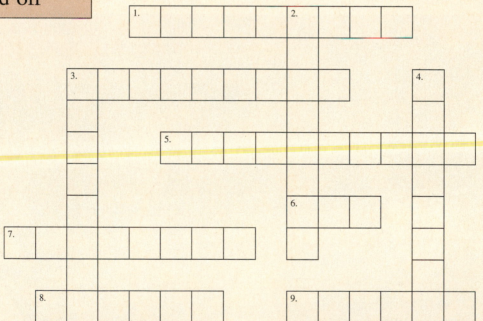

Writing Your Ideas

■ Imagine you are living in 1920. On a separate piece of paper, write a journal entry describing how you feel about women getting the right to vote.

Remembering What You Read

■ Fill in the circle next to the best ending for each sentence.

1. The 19th Amendment gave women the right to
   ○ a. fight in wars.   ○ b. make laws.   ○ c. vote.

2. "Suffs" were people who supported the
   ○ a. lawmakers.   ○ b. 19th Amendment.   ○ c. war.

3. The last state to approve the 19th Amendment was
   ○ a. Delaware.   ○ b. West Virginia.   ○ c. Tennessee.

4. Harry Burn changed his mind because of a letter from his
   ○ a. mother.   ○ b. son.   ○ c. President.

Building Skills—Use a Table

■ Use the table to answer the questions.

Women Holding Public Office in the 8 Most Populated States-1990		
	Elected to state offices	State lawmakers (legislature)
California	1	19
New York	0	23
Texas	1	19
Pennsylvania	2	17
Ohio	1	17
Florida	1	26
Illinois	0	33
Michigan	1	22
U.S.Total	46	1,273

1. What state had the most women lawmakers?_____

2. What two states had no women in state offices?_____

_____

3. How many women in these states held state offices in 1990?

_____

SAY IT AIN'T SO, JOE!

September 29, 1920—Yesterday a group of boys gathered around "Shoeless" Joe Jackson as he left the courtroom. Jackson is one of eight White Sox players charged with losing the 1919 World Series on purpose. A small boy tugged sadly at Joe's sleeve as he walked out of the room. Looking up at his hero, the boy cried, "Say it ain't so, Joe!" Jackson and two other players admitted in court that they had lost to the Cincinnati Reds on purpose. Sports fans are calling it a dark day for baseball.

Shoeless Joe Jackson at bat

The Best Team in Baseball

In 1919 the Chicago White Sox won the American League **pennant** in a breeze. This came as no surprise to baseball fans. The White Sox were clearly the best team in the league. The National League pennant was won by the Reds. This meant the White Sox and Reds would face each other in the World Series. The team that won five out of nine games would be the World Champion.

The White Sox had many star players. Shoeless Joe Jackson was their left fielder. He was one of the best hitters of all time. Claude "Lefty" Williams and Eddie "Shineball" Cicotte were great pitchers. The list went on and on.

Baseball fans felt there was no way this team could lose to the Reds. Yet strange stories were going around. A few people began whispering that the World Series was being **"fixed."** They said that some men had talked to White Sox players. These men had offered the players a lot of money to **deliberately** lose the series.

Most people didn't believe the stories. They didn't think anyone would dare fix the World Series. Still, there was one fact that troubled fans. Some people seemed to be betting a lot of money on the Reds to win.

Under a Cloud of Doubt

The first game of the World Series was played on October 1, 1919. Cicotte was pitching that day. He fell apart in the fourth inning, giving up six hits and five runs. The White Sox lost the game nine to one. *The New York Times* said the White Sox looked "like bush leaguers." In other words, they looked terrible.

The talk that the series was being fixed grew louder. Game Two didn't help. This time it was Lefty Williams who had a bad fourth inning. He gave up three walks and two hits. The final score was Reds four, White Sox two.

By this time, the World Series was under a cloud of doubt. Charles Comiskey, owner of the White Sox, felt that something was wrong. But what could he do? He had no proof that his players were trying to lose.

The Chicago White Sox in 1919

Charles Comiskey, owner of the White Sox

In the third game, the White Sox came back to win three to zero. "That's more like it," thought Comiskey. "Maybe the series isn't fixed after all. Maybe my boys were just a little nervous."

But many fans still talked about a fix. "The White Sox are just trying to make it look good," people said. "They can't let the Reds win every game. Watch what happens next."

In Game Four Cicotte again pitched. This time he started off strong. But in the fifth inning, he made two bad **errors**. This allowed the Reds to score two runs and win the game. The White Sox lost Game Five, too. Lefty Williams pitched poorly that day. The White Sox did win the next two games. But the Reds bounced back. In Game Eight they whipped the White Sox ten to five. And so the Reds won the World Series, five games to three.

The "Black Sox"

Comiskey strongly suspected that the series had been fixed. He offered $20,000 for proof of any thrown games. He said, "If we **land** the goods on any of my players, I will see that there is no place in **organized** baseball for them."

21

Comiskey made up a list of the players he thought might have fixed the series. Jackson, Cicotte, and Williams were on the list. So were George "Buck" Weaver, Arnold "Chick" Gandil, Oscar "Happy" Felsch, Charles "Swede" Risberg, and Fred McMullin. Comiskey gave the list to detectives. They spent a year trying to get proof. But they didn't find much.

In September of 1920 things changed. A **grand jury** began looking into the 1919 World Series. They talked to players, owners, and people who bet on games. Finally a man named Bill Burns admitted that he and some friends had paid eight players to lose the series. The players he named were the same ones Comiskey had on his list. On September 28, Eddie Cicotte and Lefty Williams admitted they were **guilty**. So did Shoeless Joe Jackson. The grand jury ordered all eight players to be put on trial.

Shoeless Joe Jackson

Baseball hearing in 1920

On June 27, 1921, the trial began. More than 500 fans jammed into the court. By this time, Cicotte, Jackson, and Williams had changed their stories. They now all said they were *not* guilty. Earlier they had signed papers saying they had fixed the series. But on July 22, it was learned that someone had stolen these papers. Suddenly there was no hard proof against them. On August 2, the jury found all the players not guilty. Fans in the court went wild with joy.

Sports writers and the owners of baseball teams were not as pleased. To them the White Sox had become the Black Sox. *The New York World* called the players "crooks who should not show their faces in **decent** sporting circles." Although the players had been found not guilty, baseball owners **banned** them from the Major Leagues. Not one of the eight ever set foot on a Major League field again.

Building Vocabulary

■ Match each word with its meaning.

_____ 1. deliberately

_____ 2. decent

_____ 3. organized

_____ 4. fixed

_____ 5. errors

_____ 6. banned

_____ 7. grand jury

_____ 8. land

_____ 9. pennant

_____ 10. guilty

a. did something against the law

b. flag given to top baseball team

c. proper and good

d. not allowed to do something

e. to get something

f. mistakes

g. group that decides whether to charge someone with a crime

h. on purpose

i. set up in an orderly way

j. arranged to come out in a certain way

Writing Your Ideas

■ Imagine you are a White Sox fan in 1920. On a separate sheet of paper, write a letter to a friend. Describe how you feel about the World Series being fixed.

Remembering What You Read

■ Some of the statements below are true. Others are false. Place a check in front of the three things that happened in the story.

_____ 1. Eight players refused to play in the World Series.

_____ 2. The *New York Times* said the White Sox played badly.

_____ 3. Comiskey offered $20,000 for proof of fixed games.

_____ 4. Shoeless Joe Jackson tried to lose the World Series.

_____ 5. The White Sox changed their name to Black Sox.

Thinking Critically—Fact or Opinion

■ Write **F** before each fact. Write **O** before each opinion.

_____ 1. Shoeless Joe Jackson should have been put in jail forever.

_____ 2. Charles Comiskey was the owner of the White Sox.

_____ 3. The Reds won the 1919 World Series.

_____ 4. Comiskey did not do a good job of running his team.

_____ 5. Eddie Cicotte was to blame for what happened.

_____ 6. It is silly to call men names like Lefty and Chick.

_____ 7. The jury found the players not guilty.

_____ 8. The eight players never played Major League baseball again.

GUILTY OR NOT GUILTY?

July 14, 1921—Cruel killers or good men? That is the question the court has been trying to decide for the last six weeks. Today they found Nicola Sacco and Bartolomeo Vanzetti guilty of murder. The two men will probably be sentenced to death.

But are Sacco and Vanzetti really guilty? The people of Massachusetts are deeply divided over this question. Everyone has strong ideas. Perhaps only Sacco and Vanzetti themselves know the truth.

The Crime

This story began in the small town of South Braintree, Massachusetts. It was 3:00 P.M. on April 15, 1920. Frederick Parmenter and Alessandro Berardelli were walking down Pearl Street. Each carried a metal box. The boxes held the week's pay for workers at Slater & Morrill Shoe Company. Parmenter and Berardelli were walking to the factory to pay the workers.

All at once, two men stepped out of the shadows. One pulled out a gun. He fired several shots and hit Berardelli. Parmenter tried to run away. The killers shot him as well.

Just then a black car came roaring down Pearl Street. The two killers picked up the metal boxes. One also grabbed a gun that Berardelli had been carrying. The car stopped and the killers jumped into the back seat. Both Berardelli and Parmenter died soon afterwards.

Bartolomeo Vanzetti and Nicola Sacco in court

Handcuffed together and under heavy guard, Sacco and Vanzetti walk to the courthouse.

The black car took off down Pearl Street. The killers fired wild shots at people on the street. They also dropped tacks from the car to slow down anyone who might chase them. Then the black car disappeared. It was found two days later in the woods.

The Arrest and the Trial

Police searched all over for the killers. On May 5, 1920, police **arrested** Nicola Sacco and Bartolomeo Vanzetti. Both were poor Italian Americans. Sacco worked in a shoe factory. Vanzetti sold fish from a cart in the street.

Sacco and Vanzetti were anarchists. **Anarchists** are people who believe that all governments are bad. Anarchists think the world would be better off with no one in charge. Anarchists sometimes use **violent** acts. They want to make people mad. They hope people will get mad enough to get rid of government.

The arrests were big news. Some people thought the police were heroes. Others thought they were picking on Sacco and Vanzetti because the two men held **unpopular** ideas. "Sacco and Vanzetti are guilty!" cried some people. "Sacco and Vanzetti are **innocent**!" cried others.

One hundred sixty-seven **witnesses** came forward at the trial. Some said they had seen Sacco and Vanzetti on Pearl Street just before the shootings. Others said the two men had been in different cities when the murders took place.

There were many unanswered questions. Everyone who had seen the black car on Pearl Street agreed that there were five men in the car. Who were the other three men?

The police built their case around guns. Both Sacco and Vanzetti had guns. They were carrying them when they were arrested. The bullets in Sacco's gun matched those that killed Berardelli. This made a strong case against Sacco. The case against Vanzetti was weaker. Police asked the **jury** to look at Vanzetti's gun. It looked like the one taken from Berardelli during the murders.

Supporters of Sacco and Vanzetti in London announce a protest meeting in 1927.

Rally in Union Square on August 9, 1927

The trial ended on July 14. The jury was sent to a special room. There the 12 members of the jury had to vote. They had to decide if Sacco and Vanzetti were guilty. Later a jury member told what happened. "We voted just once. There was no argument. We all agreed. Sacco and Vanzetti were guilty!"

When Sacco heard the news, he cried out, "I am innocent!"

Questions Then and Now

Sacco and Vanzetti faced the electric chair. But their **supporters** did not give up. They fought to free the two men. Some marched in front of the State House. They held signs that read "Sacco and Vanzetti Must Not Die." A few wrote books trying to prove that the two men were innocent. They asked for a new trial. Other supporters took more violent action. They blew up American buildings in places as far away as France and Cuba. They blew up the homes of the judge, a member of the jury, and a witness.

Finally, in 1927, Governor Alvan Fuller gave Sacco and Vanzetti one more chance. He asked several important people to look into the case. Known as the Lowell **Committee**, these people looked at all the facts again. They talked to the judge and the jury members. They spoke with witnesses on both sides. They even went to prison to talk to Sacco and Vanzetti. The Lowell Committee reported that there was no reason to change anything. Sacco and Vanzetti *were* guilty.

On August 23, 1927, Sacco and Vanzetti were **executed**. Nicola Sacco's last words were "Long live anarchy!" Long after they were gone, people remained interested in the case. Many talk about it even today. Some say the two men were innocent. They say Sacco and Vanzetti were found guilty because of their unpopular ideas. Other people think the two men were guilty of murder. Still others think that Sacco was guilty, but Vanzetti was innocent. Whatever the truth was, the two people who knew for sure died over 65 years ago.

Sacco and Vanzetti were found guilty.

Building Vocabulary

Part A

■ Write the best word to complete each sentence. Use each word once.

anarchists	arrested	Committee	jury

Sacco and Vanzetti were (1)_____ on May 5, 1920.

Some people thought police picked them up because they were

(2)_____. The (3)_____ found them both

guilty of murder. Later the Lowell (4)_____ agreed.

Part B

■ Fill in the circle next to the best meaning for the word in dark print.

1. He was sent to prison for his **violent** acts.
   ○ a. harmful   ○ b. kind   ○ c. greedy

2. Their ideas were **unpopular**.
   ○ a. hard to understand   ○ b. not well liked   ○ c. wrong

3. "I am **innocent**!" cried Sacco.
   ○ a. tired   ○ b. not guilty   ○ c. very sick

4. Many **witnesses** came forward.
   ○ a. people who saw something   ○ b. friends   ○ c. children

5. Their **supporters** did not give up.
   ○ a. people who help   ○ b. enemies   ○ c. lawyers

6. On August 23, 1927, Sacco and Vanzetti were **executed**.
   ○ a. excused   ○ b. put to death   ○ c. asked questions

Writing Your Ideas

■ Write three important facts you learned from this story.

Remembering What You Read

■ Find the best ending for each sentence. Fill in the circle next to it.

1. Berardelli and Parmenter were carrying a box filled with
   ○ a. tickets.　　○ b. shoes.　　○ c. money.

2. The killers escaped in a
   ○ a. plane.　　○ b. train.　　○ c. car.

3. Sacco and Vanzetti were charged with
   ○ a. kidnapping.　　○ b. murder.　　○ c. stealing a car.

4. The Lowell Committee decided Sacco and Vanzetti were
   ○ a. guilty.　　○ b. not guilty.　　○ c. not anarchists.

Building Skills—Use a Diagram

■ Use the diagram to answer the questions.

Usual Steps in a Criminal Trial

A. Arrest is made by police.

B. Grand jury decides if arrested person should be brought to trial.

C. Trial jury finds the person guilty or not guilty.

D. If guilty, punishment begins.

E. The guilty person may ask for another trial in a higher court.

1. Which jury does an arrested person face first?_____

2. When does punishment begin?_____

3. Who decides if an arrested person should be brought to trial?

4. What happens if a person is found guilty?_____

NOVARRO A STAR

August 1, 1922—Last night as the curtain fell in the Astor Theater, a star was born! His name is Ramón Novarro. Novarro sparkled as he played Rupert in *The Prisoner of Zenda*.

The movie, which opened in New York City, was a big hit. As people left the theater, many were talking about Novarro. Some think that this young actor from Mexico will be a star for years to come.

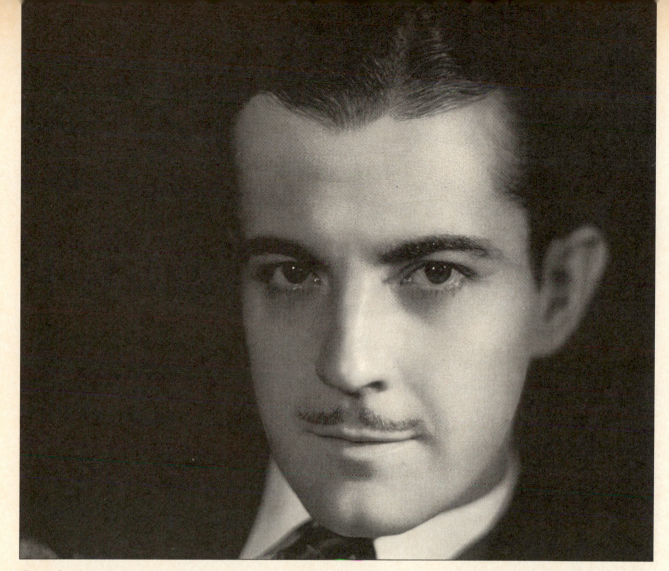

Ramón Novarro

From Mexico to California

Ramón Novarro was born in Durango, Mexico, in 1899. His real name was José Ramón Gil Samaniegos. Ramón's father was a dentist. The Samaniegos had money for private schools and special teachers. Ramón dreamed of becoming an American movie star. His **future** looked bright.

But when Ramón was 14, his life changed. Trouble broke out in Mexico. Mexican leaders were fighting for control of the country. Suddenly Ramón's family did not feel safe. Like many others, they left their home and **fled** to the United States.

Hanging on to His Dreams

The Samaniegos moved to Los Angeles, California. American life was hard for them. The language and **customs** were different. They had no money. To make things worse, Mr. Samaniegos became very ill. Ramón got a job to support the family.

Ramón had many different jobs. He served food in a restaurant. Then he worked as a clerk in a grocery store and as a piano teacher. But Ramón hung on to his dream of becoming an actor. He practiced his performing skills. He sang in small clubs and restaurants. He also **brushed up** on his dancing. In 1917 he started to get work as an **extra** in movies.

The next year, Ramón was performing full-time. He joined a dance company. He traveled through Canada with this group. The head of the company saw how good Ramón was. She helped him get work as a dancer in several movies.

Ramón was **grateful** for this help. "But I don't just want to dance," he thought. "I want to *act*." Every time Ramón showed up for his dance scenes, he talked to the **directors**. He told them how much he wanted to be an actor.

Novarro in *Ben Hur* in 1927

36

Novarro in *Scaramouche*

A Big Break

At last Ramón got his big break. A famous director named Rex Ingram was making *The Prisoner of Zenda*. The movie told the story of two men, Michael and Rupert, who want to run the country. They **kidnap** the king and keep him a prisoner in the castle of Zenda. Ingram asked Ramón to play the **role** of the **sly** and handsome Rupert.

"I also want you to change your name," Ingram told him.

"You need a name that sounds handsome and is easy to remember. Instead of being Ramón Samaniegos, you will be Ramón Novarro." Ramón agreed.

When the movie opened in 1922, Ramón became a star. His dreamy look made people fond of him. Ingram offered Ramón parts in other movies. By the late 1920s, Ramón was earning $10,000 a week. His dream had come true. He was an American movie star.

37

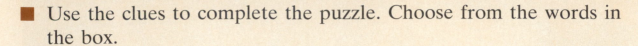

■ Use the clues to complete the puzzle. Choose from the words in the box.

role
directors
grateful
sly
extra
brushed up
fled
kidnap
future
customs

Across

6. people who guide actors
7. an actor who has a small part
8. time yet to come
9. smart and sneaky
10. ran away

Down

1. capture and hold someone
2. the part an actor plays
3. ways of doing things
4. thankful
5. practiced

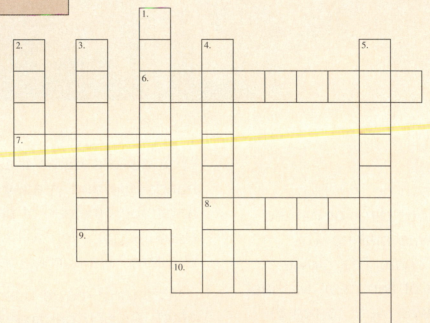

Writing Your Ideas

■ Imagine you are Ramón Novarro. On a separate sheet of paper, write a short speech you will give to young people. Tell why it is important to hang on to your dreams.

Remembering What You Read

■ Some of the statements below are true. Others are false. Place a check in front of the three things that happened in the story.

_____ 1. Ramón Novarro changed his name to Rupert Zenda.

_____ 2. The Samaniegos moved from Mexico to the United States.

_____ 3. Ramón Novarro broke his leg dancing.

_____ 4. Ramón told directors he wanted to act.

_____ 5. Novarro became a star in *The Prisoner of Zenda*.

Thinking Critically—Cause and Effect

1. The Samaniegos left Mexico because _____

_____

_____

2. Ramón had to support his family in Los Angeles because

_____

_____

3. The head of the dance company helped Ramon get work because

_____

_____

4. Ramón was not happy just being a dancer because _____

_____

_____

5. Ramón used the name Novarro because _____

_____

_____

KING TUT'S TOMB FOUND!

November 3, 1922—Today, Howard Carter may have made the most important discovery in all of Egypt. For many years Carter has been digging in Egypt's "Valley of the Kings." He has been searching for old treasures in graves of Egyptian kings. At last, Carter may have found what he's been searching for—a grave which hasn't been emptied by robbers. The treasure in this grave could tell the world much about the Egypt of 3,000 years ago.

The Boy-King

The **tomb** that Carter found belonged to the **ancient** King Tutankhamen. Tutankhamen was not a great Egyptian king. He ruled only a few years, from 1361 B.C. to 1352 B.C He was just a child when he took the throne. And he died at the age of 17 or 18.

When Tutankhamen died, the people of ancient Egypt put his body in a gold **coffin**. They carried the **sealed** coffin to the Valley of the Kings. There he would join all the other Egyptian kings. They put his body in a tomb. They also put jewels and other **valuables** in the tomb. Then the tomb was sealed. The body of the dead king was left in peace. Egyptians believed keeping Tut's body safe would allow his spirit to join the gods.

Gold mask of King Tutankhamen

Many royal tombs were found in the Valley of the Kings.

The Search for the Tomb

Thirty-three royal tombs had been discovered in the Valley of the Kings. These tombs were 3,000 years old. Some were built for famous kings such as Rameses II. Others were for less important leaders. All the tombs had been opened by thieves. The thieves had stolen or destroyed most of the riches inside. Some had been robbed soon after they were built. Others were broken into hundreds of years later. Modern **archeologists** found few things remaining in the tombs.

Howard Carter studied a list of the ancient kings. Most of their tombs had been found.

But Carter believed there was still one more tomb in the Valley of the Kings. This was the tomb of King Tutankhamen, or King "Tut" as modern writers call him. Since King Tut was not well-known, Carter hoped that his tomb had not been found by robbers. He hoped it still contained all the things that had been buried with the king.

There was one problem. No one knew where King Tut's tomb was. In fact, no one was sure it even **existed**. Perhaps robbers had destroyed it completely. Or perhaps it was covered by dirt so that the tomb would never be found.

Carter did not have much money. For 15 years, a rich man named Lord Carnarvon had paid for his digging. But by 1922, Carnarvon was tired of Carter's search. A fortune was spent and there was nothing to show for it. "I will pay for no more digging," he told Carter.

Carter understood Carnarvon's feelings. But he was not ready to give up. He showed his **sponsor** a map of the Valley of the Kings. "Look," he said to Carnarvon, "I have searched almost the whole Valley. There is only one small place where we have not dug." Carter pointed out a small spot on the map. "Give me a few more months to dig here. If I find nothing, I will give up. I will know that the Valley of the Kings has no more secrets."

A gold panel that was found in King Tut's tomb

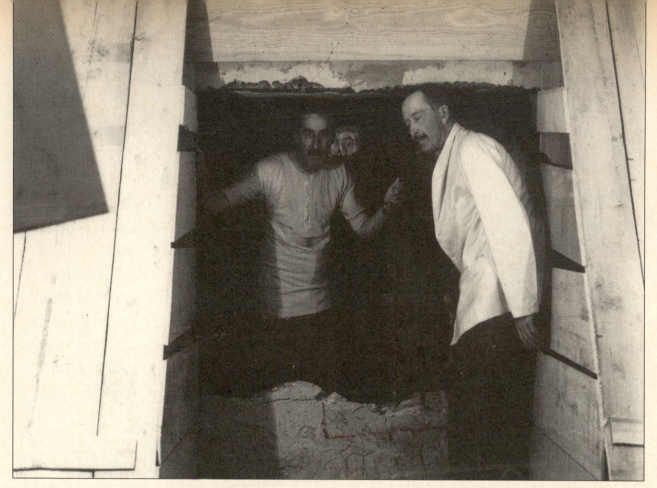

Lord Carnarvon and Howard Carter at opening of King Tut's tomb

Lord Carnarvon agreed. By November 1, 1922, Carter was back at work. He and his workers chipped away rock by rock. Suddenly on the afternoon of November 3, some workers called to Carter. He came rushing over. In front of him lay a hole the workers had dug. The hole showed a step leading down into the ground.

"It seemed almost too good to be true . . ." wrote Carter later. But these were the steps to King Tut's tomb.

What Lies Within?

Carter was thrilled. But he knew he had to be careful. He could not just rush into the tomb. He might break something that lay inside.

Carter sent word of the exciting discovery to Lord Carnarvon. He posted guards all around the area to keep out robbers. Then he slowly began to dig toward the tomb.

By November 24, the steps to the tomb had been cleared. Carter was ready to open the tomb itself. Lord Carnarvon had come to watch. Both men were nervous. They did not know what to expect.

With trembling hands, Carter pulled at a corner of the door.

The stones fell away. Carter held a candle up to the hole. He looked inside.

"Can you see anything?" asked Carnarvon.

For a moment Carter could say nothing. Then he whispered "Yes, wonderful things . . ."

What Carter saw was the **brilliant** glow of gold. Gold objects lay everywhere in the tomb. King Tut's tomb had *not* been emptied! Robbers had not found it. Howard Carter was the first person in thousands of years to enter Tut's tomb.

Carter spent the next six years digging out the tomb. All four rooms were filled with treasures. In one room Carter found the body of Tutankhamen himself, wrapped in his gold coffin. In all, nearly 5,000 **items** were found in the tomb. It was the greatest Egyptian treasure ever discovered. Howard Carter had uncovered the last secret of the Valley of the Kings.

Some of the 5,000 items found in the tomb

Building Vocabulary

■ To complete the sentences choose a word from the box. Write the word on the blanks after the sentence. The letters in the boxes will spell the answer to number 10.

valuables	existed	sealed	coffin	tomb
archeologists	sponsor	items	ancient	

1. Egyptians buried
   _____ with kings.   ▯
   __ __ __ __ ▯ __ __ __

2. Lord Carnarvon was
   Carter's _____.   ▯
   __ __ __ __ __ ▯

3. No one was sure
   King Tut's tomb _____.   ▯
   __ __ __ __ ▯ __ __ __

4. Egyptians _____
   King Tut's coffin.   ▯
   __ __ __ ▯ __ __

5. Modern _____
   searched the Valley. __ __ __ __ __ __ ▯ __ __ __ __ __

6. Over 5,000 _____
   were found.   ▯
   __ __ __ __ __

7. King Tut was an
   _____ king.   ▯
   __ __ __ __ __ __

8. King Tut's body was
   in a gold _____.   __ __ __ __ __ ▯

9. King Tut's _____
   was found in 1922.   ▯
   __ __ __

10. The glow of the gold in the tomb was _____.

Writing Your Ideas

■ Imagine you are a reporter who was there when King Tut's tomb was first opened. On a separate sheet of paper, write a news story describing the event.

Remembering What You Read

■ Answer the questions.

1. Who was Tutankhamen? _____

_____

2. How did Lord Carnarvon help Howard Carter? _____

_____

3. Who had destroyed most of the tombs in the Valley of the Kings?

_____

4. What did Carter see when he first opened King Tut's tomb?

_____

Building Skills—Use a Map

■ Use the map to answer the following questions.

1. What three ancient places are listed on the map?

_____

_____

_____

2. What two seas are shown on the map?

_____

_____

3. What direction is the Valley of the Kings from Cairo?

_____

4. Which modern city is near the Mediterranean Sea?

_____

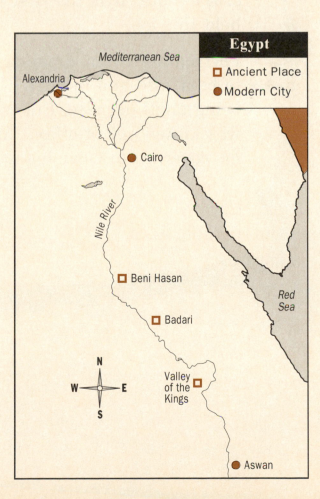

Egypt
□ Ancient Place
● Modern City

Mediterranean Sea

Alexandria

Cairo

Nile River

Beni Hasan

Badari

Red Sea

Valley of the Kings

Aswan

N W E S

HE'S OUT, BUT SHE'S IN!

November 4, 1924—Ma Ferguson is the new governor of Texas! The woman who loves to grow flowers and feed chickens has just become head of the state. It is the first time a woman has ever held this job.

For years Miriam Amanda Ferguson was happy to be a wife and mother. She had no dreams of being anything else. But when her husband Jim was kicked out of office, "Ma" got mad. She ran for governor to clear his name.

Jim and Miriam Ferguson

The Rise and Fall of a Governor

Miriam Amanda Wallace grew up in Bell County, Texas. After going to college, she married Jim Ferguson. Jim was a country boy with big plans. In 1914 he ran for governor. No one expected him to win. But Jim knew how to talk to Texas farmers. He promised he would fight for their rights. To the surprise of many, "Farmer Jim" won the race.

As governor, Jim was always in the news. Miriam was happy to stay in the **background**. She was a gentle woman who liked to cook and garden. She enjoyed taking care of her two daughters.

In 1917 the Fergusons' lives changed. Jim found himself in big trouble. Farmers and poor people liked him. But others did not. He had angered many **powerful** people. These people took a close look at "Farmer Jim."

49

They found that Jim had "borrowed" money which belonged to the state. He had not returned it. They also said private companies had loaned him $156,000. People wondered what Jim had agreed to do in return for the money. These were serious **charges**. If they were true, Jim was guilty of breaking the law.

That summer state lawmakers **impeached** Jim. They said he had not acted the way a governor should. Jim was found guilty of wrong actions. He was ordered to leave office. He was told he could not hold office in Texas again.

Jim spent the next seven years fighting for his **career**. He asked the courts to let him run for office again. But in 1924 the Texas **Supreme Court** ruled against him. It looked like Jim Ferguson was out of Texas politics forever.

A Crazy Idea

Jim did not know what to do. Neither did Miriam. The **public** life they had planned was over. One night they sat talking in their living room. Slowly an idea came to them. "You can't run for governor again," Miriam told Jim. "But I can."

Ma Ferguson signs a bill.

Ma Ferguson was elected governor again in 1932.

It seemed like a crazy idea at first. No woman had ever been governor of a state. Besides, Miriam had never been interested in politics. But Jim would be there to help her. "It's the only way to clear our family name," Miriam said.

Me for Ma

So the Fergusons announced that Miriam would run. "You'll get two governors for the price of one," they told people. Reporters often used Miriam's **initials** (M. A.) in stories about her. One reporter shortened this to "Ma". Miriam did not like this **nickname**. But everyone else did. Supporters began carrying signs which read "Me for Ma."

The same people who had voted for "Farmer Jim" now supported Ma Ferguson. She was seen as a hero of ordinary people. Newspapers printed pictures of her at home **canning** peaches. Poor farmers rushed to vote for her. When the votes were counted, Ma Ferguson won easily. The people of Texas had returned the Fergusons to power.

Building Vocabulary

■ Match each word with its meaning.

_____ 1. Supreme Court

_____ 2. impeached

_____ 3. canning

_____ 4. nickname

_____ 5. initials

_____ 6. powerful

_____ 7. public

_____ 8. background

_____ 9. charges

_____ 10. career

a. statements saying that a person has broken the law

b. having to do with government

c. highest court in the state or country

d. the work a person does through life

e. what is behind something else

f. a name used instead of a real name

g. strong and important

h. accused a person in office of acting in a wrong way

i. putting food into a jar to store it for a very long time.

j. first letters of names

Writing Your Ideas

■ Imagine that you are either Miriam or Jim Ferguson. You have just heard that "Ma" has won the election. On a separate sheet of paper, write a journal entry describing how you feel.

Remembering What You Read

■ Fill in the circle next to the best ending for each sentence.

1. Jim Ferguson was well liked by
   ○ a. farmers.   ○ b. rich people.   ○ c. students.

2. State lawmakers found that Jim Ferguson had
   ○ a. lost his mind.   ○ b. broken the law.
   ○ c. won a prize.

3. Miriam Ferguson decided to run for
   ○ a. president.   ○ b. Supreme Court.   ○ c. governor.

4. Miriam was given the nickname "Ma" by
   ○ a. her mother.   ○ b. Jim Ferguson.   ○ c. a reporter.

5. Jim left office because
   ○ a. he was guilty of wrong actions.
   ○ b. he wanted to leave politics.
   ○ c. he thought it was his wife's turn to be governor.

Thinking Critically—Sequence

■ Number the sentences to show the order in which things happened in the story. The first one is done for you.

_____ Jim Ferguson became governor of Texas.

_____ Ma Ferguson became governor of Texas.

_____ Jim Ferguson was found guilty of wrong actions.

__1__ Miriam Amanda Wallace married Jim Ferguson.

_____ People carried signs that read "Me for Ma."

"MONKEY TRIAL" BEGINS TODAY!

July 10, 1925—A hot summer sun will bake the town of Dayton, Tennessee again today. But the hottest place in town is likely to be the courthouse. This is where John Scopes goes on trial. Scopes is a teacher at Central High School. He is charged with teaching evolution. Teaching evolution is against the law in Tennessee.

Testing the Evolution Law

For many years **evolution** was not a popular idea. In 1859 Charles Darwin had published a paper about evolution. In his paper Darwin said human beings developed from lower forms of life. Over millions of years on Earth, lower life forms developed into higher ones. This led to the evolution of monkeys and then, finally, humans.

Many people made fun of this idea. People were upset that schools might be teaching that humans came "from a lower **order** of animals." They wanted a law against teaching about evolution. The law was passed in March of 1925.

Some people believed the 1925 law was wrong. They thought Darwin's ideas were important. The **Darwinists** decided to fight the law. First, they had to find a teacher willing to break the law. Then the law could be tested in court. The Darwinists hoped the court would agree that the law was wrong.

John Scopes was brought to trial for teaching evolution.

55

Clarence Darrow and William Jennings Bryan

A teacher named John Thomas Scopes agreed to help. One day he taught about evolution in his high-school science class. Later, Scopes was arrested for breaking the law. William Jennings Bryan would fight the case against Scopes. Clarence Darrow, the country's most famous lawyer, offered to **defend** Scopes.

Two Heroes

William Jennings Bryan was 65 years old when the case came to trial. He was a **Creationist** and was ready to fight for what he believed.

Bryan taught Bible classes. He taught that everything in the Bible was true. He taught that the Bible's words meant exactly what they said.

To Bryan the whole idea of evolution was wrong. Bryan was famous for speaking out about his ideas. Many people had heard him speak. When he arrived in Dayton, he was greeted as a hero.

When the trial began, Clarence Darrow was 68 years old. He, too, was seen as a hero. Darrow had spent his life fighting for the poor and the weak. Like Bryan, he believed in the Bible. Unlike Bryan, he also believed in evolution.

Darrow Against Bryan

People came to Dayton to see the two lawyers battle. People acted almost as if the circus had come to town. Everyone wanted to see the sparks fly. People made signs to show which side they were on. Most people supported Bryan.

Store owners in Dayton saw a chance to do more business. They used the monkey idea to get people into their stores. One owner made a sign saying, "Don't monkey around when you come to Dayton—come to us." Another sign read, "We handle every kind of meat except monkey."

Bryan made his case quickly. He **called** two high-school students into court. Each said that Scopes had talked about evolution in class. Bryan then felt his work was done. He had shown that Scopes broke the law.

Then it was Darrow's turn. He asked the judge if he could question **experts** in science and the Bible. Darrow wanted to show that people could believe in the Bible *and* evolution. But the judge said no. "The only question," he said, "is whether Scopes broke the law."

Many people came to Dayton to see the court battle.

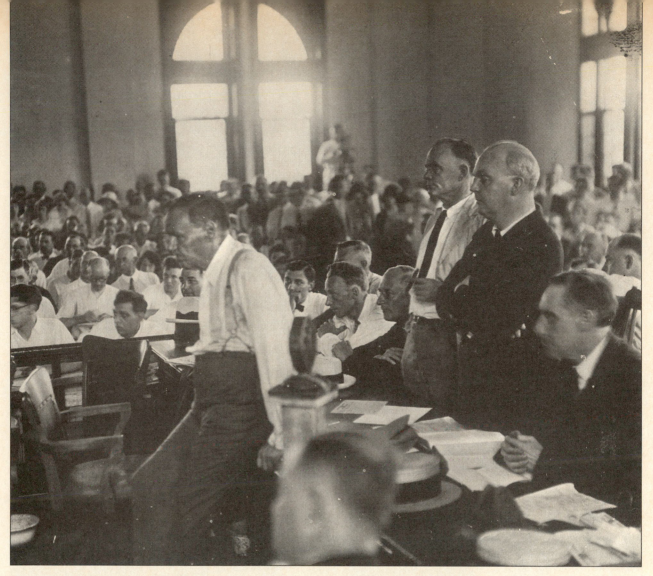

Clarence Darrow leans against a desk as he listens to testimony.

It looked like Darrow would lose. Clearly Scopes had broken the law. Darrow could not change that. Some reporters left town. They decided the story was over.

Then William Jennings Bryan made a mistake. He agreed to take the stand as an expert on the Bible. Bryan did not have to do this. But he wanted to prove that he was right and Darrow was wrong.

As Bryan took his seat, the crowd cheered. The courtroom was hot and stuffy. But no one seemed to care. This was the moment they had waited for—a fight between Bryan and Darrow.

Bryan waved a large fan back and forth to cool his face. Darrow asked him about some statements in the Bible. Was Jonah swallowed by a whale? Was Eve made from one of Adam's rib's? Darrow asked if the statements in the Bible were true word for word. Bryan became confused. He couldn't answer the questions.

For two hours, Darrow **pressed** Bryan harder and harder. Bryan waved his fan faster and faster. He was no match for Darrow. Darrow asked questions about science. But Bryan knew little about the subject. Slowly the crowd **turned** on Bryan. They laughed at some of his answers. William Jennings Bryan, the great speaker, no longer knew what to say.

The next day the trial ended. Scopes was found guilty. He was **fined** $100. In spite of the verdict, Darrow and his supporters felt they had really won.

Because of the "monkey trial," only two other states passed laws against evolution. In 1968 the Supreme Court struck down these laws. Teachers in every state could talk freely about the ideas of Charles Darwin.

William Jennings Bryan gives his views.

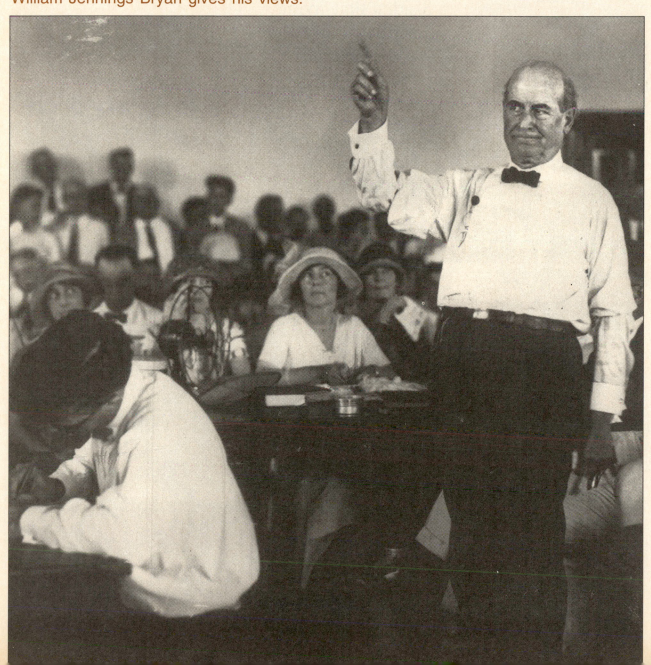

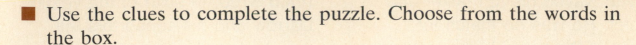

Building Vocabulary

■ Use the clues to complete the puzzle. Choose from the words in the box.

evolution
defend
called
Creationist
order
pressed
Darwinists
fined
turned
experts

Across

1. ask someone to come

4. suddenly became unfriendly toward

7. punished by being made to pay money

8. idea that living things slowly develop from simpler forms of life

9. group of plants or animals that share some features

10. person who believes the Bible story of how the world was made

Down

2. people who believe in Darwin's idea of evolution

3. push a person to do something

5. people who know a lot about a subject

6. act to protect someone

Writing Your Ideas

■ On a separate sheet of paper, write three important facts you learned from this story.

Remembering What You Read

■ Answer the questions.

1. Why was John Scopes brought to court? _____

   _____

2. Who was Scopes' lawyer? _____

3. How did William Jennings Bryan feel about evolution? _____

   _____

4. What happened when Darrow asked Bryan questions about

   the Bible? _____

   _____

Building Skills—Read a Graph

■ Use the graph to answer the questions.

1. What three religious groups
   are shown on the graph?

   _____

   _____

   _____

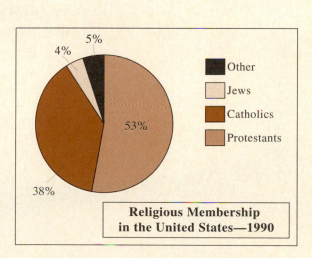

4% 5%

Other
Jews
Catholics
Protestants

53%

38%

**Religious Membership
in the United States—1990**

2. This graph shows information
   about what country?

   _____

3. In the United States, what religious group has the most members?

   _____

4. What percentage of religious members in the U.S. are Jews?

   _____

SLEEPING CAR PORTERS UNITE

August 25, 1925—A handful of railroad men gathered at a Harlem meeting hall today. The men are sleeping car porters for the Pullman Company. The porters work long hours for low pay. They met today to form their own labor union. The porters hope the union will help them get more pay and shorter hours. The Pullman Company has threatened to fire any porter who joins a union.

A railroad official inspects sleeping car porters.

Working on the Railroad

In the 1920s life was **grim** for the African Americans who worked as sleeping car porters. Their job was to keep sleeping cars clean and in good order. The porters also took care of the passengers who rode in the cars. Sleeping car porters served meals. They shined passengers' shoes. They did their best to **accommodate** the passengers' needs.

Sleeping car porters were always **on call**. Day or night, passengers could call a porter just by ringing a bell. Porters were lucky to get three or four hours of sleep at night.

For all their hard work, porters were paid very little. The Pullman Company paid porters only 26 cents an hour. Each month they worked up to 400 hours. They traveled about 11,000 miles. At that rate a porter should have made over $100 a month. Yet most porters earned only $67.50 a month. How could this be? Porters were not paid for all the hours they worked. They spent up to five hours a day getting sleeping cars ready for travel. But the men were only paid for work while the train was moving.

Randolph Leads the Way

A man named Asa Philip Randolph wanted to help the porters. Randolph was the son of two **former** slaves. He had **devoted** himself to fighting for African American workers. In 1917 he had started his own magazine. It was called the *Messenger*. The magazine spoke out for the rights of African Americans. Almost all porters were African American.

Randolph thought sleeping car porters should have shorter hours and more pay. He also thought they should be treated with **respect**. He was angry that many people called all porters "George."

Too many passengers did not bother to learn their porter's real name. As Randolph later wrote, porters **deserved** to be treated "like men and not like children."

"What the porters need," Randolph said, "is a union of their own. All the other railroad workers have unions. Why not the porters?" A few brave men agreed with Randolph. On August 25, 1925, they met with him to form a union. They called it the Brotherhood of Sleeping Car Porters. Within seven months 5,000 of the 12,000 porters had joined the union.

First Pullman sleeping car and Asa Philip Randolph, President of the Brotherhood of Sleeping Porters

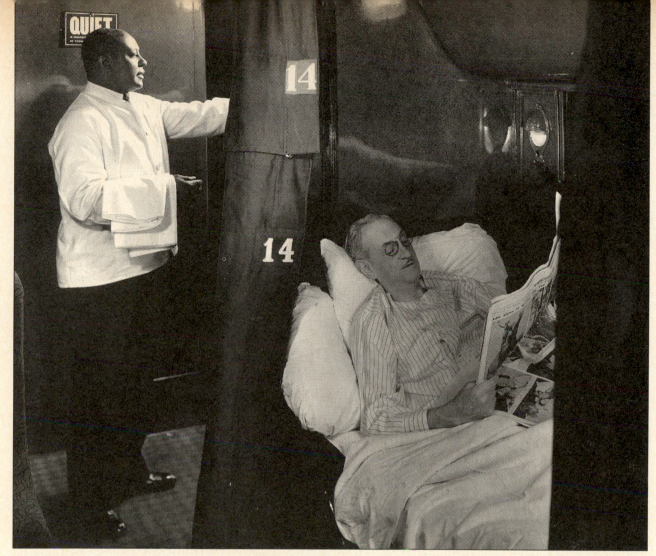

Sleeping car porters were always on call.

A Long Struggle

The new union did not make wild **demands**. It asked only for a little more pay and shorter hours. But the Pullman Company refused to deal with the group. In fact it tried to destroy the union. The company fired any porter who was known to be a union member. Some porters were paid to spy on others. The message was clear— *Quit the union or lose your job.*

Afraid of losing their jobs, most union members quit. But Randolph would not let the union die. He fought for the union in court. And finally, things began to change. In the 1930s, new laws were passed. These laws forced companies to accept unions. On August 25, 1937—exactly 12 years after the union was formed—the Pullman Company agreed to **bargain** with the Brotherhood of Sleeping Car Porters. A few months later, a **contract** was signed which gave porters shorter hours and better pay. Randolph's hard work and the porters' courage had finally paid off.

Building Vocabulary

■ Match each word with its meaning.

_____ 1. on call   a. try to work out the terms of a deal

_____ 2. devoted   b. show honor to someone

_____ 3. accommodate   c. gave time and attention

_____ 4. bargain   d. ready to work whenever needed

_____ 5. respect   e. was worthy of something

_____ 6. demands   f. statements of what you feel you must have

_____ 7. deserved   g. go out of your way to help someone

Part B

■ Read each sentence. Fill in the circle next to the best meaning for the word in dark print. You may use the glossary.

1. Life for sleeping car porters was **grim**.
   ○ a. difficult   ○ b. always the same   ○ c. boring

2. Randolph was the son of **former** slaves.
   ○ a. important   ○ b. past   ○ c. women

3. The porters signed a **contract**.
   ○ a. high wall   ○ b. written agreement   ○ c. angry letter

Writing Your Ideas

■ Imagine you are a sleeping car porter in the 1920s. On a separate sheet of paper, write a letter to a friend describing a day's work.

Remembering What You Read

■ Some of the statements below are true. Others are false. Place a check in front of the three things that happened in the story.

_____ 1. Sleeping car porters worked up to 400 hours a month.

_____ 2. Sleeping car porters formed a union.

_____ 3. Asa Philip Randolph bought the Pullman Company.

_____ 4. The Brotherhood of Sleeping Car Porters fired Randolph.

_____ 5. New laws were passed which forced companies to accept unions.

Thinking Critically—Main Ideas

■ Underline the two most important ideas from the story.

1. Sleeping car porters served meals on trains.

2. The union helped sleeping car porters.

3. Asa Philip Randolph was the son of two former slaves.

4. In the 1920s, sleeping car porters were treated poorly.

5. Passengers could call sleeping car porters by ringing a bell.

6. The sleeping car porters were paid for every minute they were on the train.

FIRST ROCKET FIRED!

March 16, 1926—In a snow-covered field near Auburn, Massachusetts, Robert Goddard fired the world's first modern rocket. Goddard watched as the rocket rose through the cold winter air.

Goddard believes rockets are the first step in space travel. "Someday," he said, "rockets will put people on the moon."

Experiments That Failed

Growing up in Massachusetts in the 1880s, Robert dreamed of flying. No one had ever done it. Airplanes had not yet been **invented**. But young Robert felt sure that machines could help people fly.

Robert himself tried several experiments in flying. He experimented with a battery, hot-air balloon, and shooting arrows. All the experiments failed. Still, Robert searched for a way that people could fly.

A Different Person

One day when Robert was 17, something amazing happened. As he later wrote, "On the afternoon of October 19, 1899, I climbed a tall cherry tree at the back of the barn . . ." There Robert looked out over the hay fields. Suddenly he had an idea. What if people could find a way to travel in space? What if they could fly to Mars? He wrote, "I imagined how wonderful it would be to make some **device** that had the possibility of flying to Mars . . ."

Robert Goddard as a ten-year-old boy with his parents

69

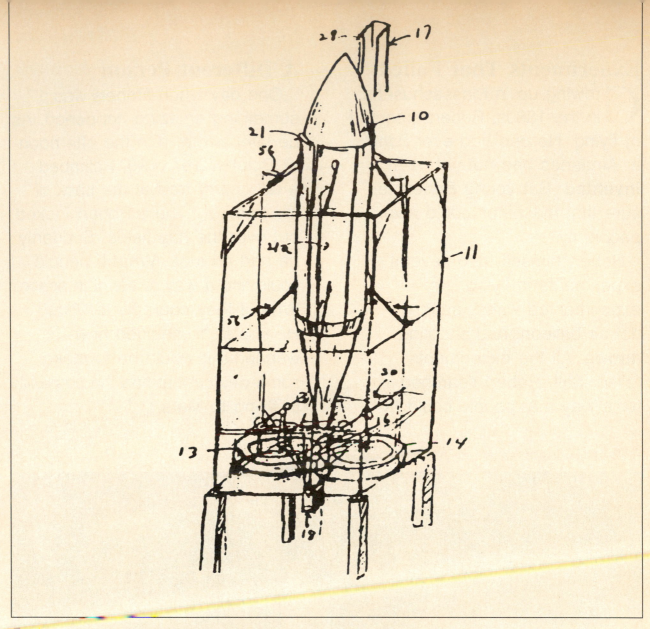

Goddard drew this sketch of a rocket in one of his early notebooks.

By the time Robert climbed down from the tree, he felt like "a different person." He knew what he wanted to do with his life. He wanted to build rockets that could fly in space.

Soon Robert began to keep secret notebooks. He wrote down his thoughts about space travel. He also wrote down ideas for building **spacecraft**.

Robert became a teacher. He spent all his free time trying to develop a rocket that would work. Year after year, he studied and experimented.

Every year on October 19, he went back out to the cherry tree behind the barn. He called it "**Anniversary** Day." There he reminded himself of his dream. "Someday," he thought, "a rocket *will* fly to the moon."

The Test

By 1913 Robert Goddard had thought of a new way to power a rocket. He would use liquid fuel. Robert was excited. He began running tests with this fuel. But before he could finish the tests, he became sick. Robert went to see doctors. They discovered that he had a disease called tuberculosis. This sickness was attacking his **lungs**. Robert's doctors sadly told him, "You only have two weeks to live."

Robert lay in bed, not moving. One week passed, then two. A month went by. Robert Goddard was still sick, but he was alive. His body was winning the fight against tuberculosis! Slowly Robert grew stronger. He began writing in his notebooks again. By 1915 he was back at work.

Robert Goddard teaching in 1924

One night Robert had a dream. He dreamed he was flying to the moon. The next day he drew a picture of the spacecraft that took him there. In 1969 people really did land on the moon. They landed in a spaceship that looked very much like the one Robert Goddard drew.

Robert continued his work on rockets. At last, on March 16, 1926, he was ready to try firing one. He carried a ten-foot rocket out into a snowy field near Auburn, Massachusetts. His wife, Esther, went with him. She brought a movie camera to record the flight.

Robert later told what happened when the rocket was lit. "The rocket did not rise at first, but the flame came out. There was a **steady** roar. After a number of seconds it rose, slowly and then at express-train speed. It looked almost magical as it rose. It rose 41 feet and then went sideways 184 feet in 2.5 seconds. . . ."

Goddard tests the world's first modern rocket.

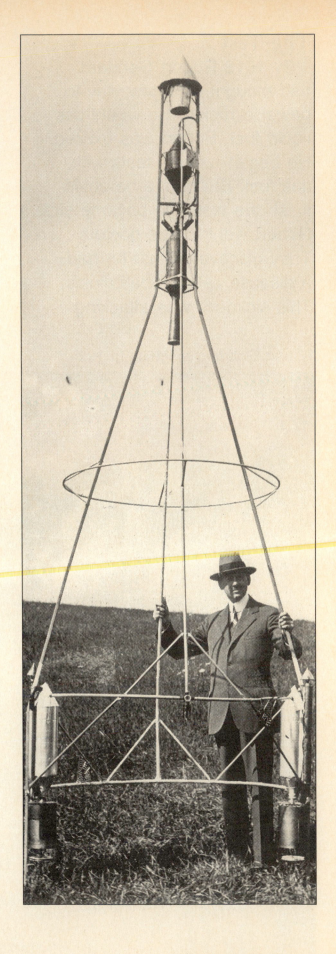

Full-Time Work

The first modern rocket had gotten off the ground! The flight was a success! Robert continued his experiments. In 1930, after 30 years of **struggling** on his own, a large foundation finally offered to pay for Robert's **research**. At last, he could give all his time to rockets. He needed empty land and good weather for his experiments. So Robert, Esther, and four **assistants** moved to a ranch in New Mexico. There they continued to make and test rockets.

In spite of his many successes, Robert received little support for his ideas. Most people were just getting used to airplanes. They couldn't imagine something that could travel in space. When he died in August 1945, Goddard still had not been recognized as the **pioneer** he was.

Goddard was responsible for 241 inventions. These inventions were used in building the spacecraft that traveled to the moon and to Mars. Only after his death, did Robert Goddard become known as the "Father of Rockets."

Goddard and four assistants hold a rocket in 1932.

Building Vocabulary

■ Write the best word to complete each sentence. Use each word once.

pioneer	spacecraft	research

Robert Goddard was a (1)_____ in the field of modern

rockets. He spent many years doing (2)_____ on rockets.

His work helped send (3)_____ to the moon and to Mars.

Part B

■ Match each word with its meaning.

_____ 1. device   a. people who help

_____ 2. assistants   b. working very hard

_____ 3. invented   c. part of the body used for breathing

_____ 4. anniversary   d. not changing

_____ 5. struggling   e. machine made for a certain use

_____ 6. lungs   f. made for the first time

_____ 7. steady   g. day of the year when something important once happened

Writing Your Ideas

■ Robert Goddard spent his life trying to make his dream come true. On a separate sheet of paper, write about a dream you might like to come true.

74

Remembering What You Read

■ Fill in the circle next to the best ending for each sentence.

1. Robert Goddard dreamed of flying to
   ○ a. California.   ○ b. the moon and Mars.   ○ c. the sun.

2. Tuberculosis made Robert very
   ○ a. rich.   ○ b. smart.   ○ c. sick.

3. Robert Goddard built a rocket that used
   ○ a. liquid fuel.   ○ b. too much fuel.   ○ c. no fuel.

4. Robert Goddard's inventions helped people go to
   ○ a. space.   ○ b. sleep.   ○ c. school.

Building Skills—Use a Time Line

■ Use the time line to answer the questions.

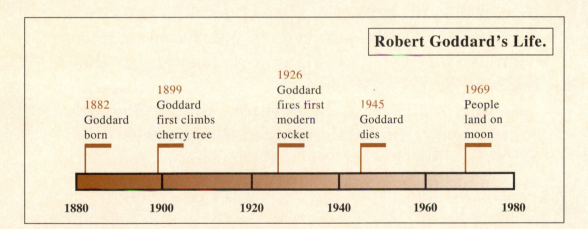

1. When did Robert Goddard first climb the cherry tree?_____

_____

2. Was Robert Goddard alive when people landed on the moon?

_____

3. Put a mark on the time line to show when Robert Goddard became sick with tuberculosis.

4. Circle the year that Robert Goddard was born.

WORLD'S FIRST TALKING CARTOON

November 18, 1928—Everybody is talking about *Steamboat Willie*! People saw this Walt Disney cartoon today for the first time. Many were laughing as they left New York City's Colony Theater. "It knocked me out of my seat!" cried one reporter. "Bright! Snappy! A good deal of fun!" said another. What makes *Steamboat Willie* so special? It's the first cartoon ever made with sound.

Mickey Mouse as Steamboat Willie

An Idea Takes Shape

In the early 1920s, all **films** were silent. People also watched silent cartoons. Walt Disney had made two silent cartoon series. But like many people, he thought the **characters** in cartoons were not very interesting. "I need to think of a better character," Disney thought.

In 1928 the 26-year-old Disney was riding a train. Suddenly an idea came to him. "I could see a **merry** little figure," Disney said.

The idea was **vague** at first. But the idea grew and developed. Finally Disney had his character— a mouse. He would draw a **romping** little mouse.

Disney drew this mouse with big round ears and **enormous** shoes. At first, Disney wanted to call the mouse Mortimer. But Disney's wife, Lilly, thought the name was too long. "How about Mickey?" she said. "It's short and friendly." So the character became "Mickey Mouse."

Talking Movies

To start, Disney made two silent cartoons about Mickey Mouse. One was called *Plane Crazy*. The other was *Gallopin' Gaucho*. Both turned out well. About that same time, something happened which shook the whole movie business. *The Jazz Singer* **opened** in New York City. People rushed to see it. *The Jazz Singer* was the world's first "talking" movie. Some people thought talking movies were just a **fad**.

Walt Disney knew better. He was sure that sound was here to stay. So Disney went to work on a talking Mickey Mouse cartoon.

Mickey Speaks!

The cartoon was *Steamboat Willie*. It was drawn and put together as a silent cartoon. Then music and voice were added. Disney worked hard to match the sound to the cartoon. Finally, he got the sound just right. In the fall of 1928, the cartoon was finished.

Walt Disney poses with his popular new character.

A scene from the first talking movie, *The Jazz Singer*

In the cartoon, Mickey Mouse makes sounds in a funny, high-**pitched** voice. The voice belonged to Walt Disney. When he talked about his cartoons, Disney would sometimes pretend to be Mickey. The high squeaky voice he used always made people laugh. Disney hoped his squeaky sounds would now help to make *Steamboat Willie* a success.

Disney took his new cartoon to big movie companies. They liked it, but no one would buy the cartoon. Finally the **manager** of New York's Colony Theater agreed to show it for two weeks. "Those big companies don't know what they want," the manager told Disney. "They need to hear how great it is from movie fans."

The manager was right. Huge crowds gathered to see *Steamboat Willie*. In only two weeks, the big movie companies changed their minds. Over time Mickey Mouse became a household word. In fact, in 1988, Mickey Mouse celebrated 60 years as a cartoon star. Disney was right. Sound was here to stay.

Building Vocabulary

■ To complete the sentences choose a word from the box. Write the word on the blanks after the sentence. The letters will tell you what Mickey Mouse became.

| vague | enormous | opened | pitched | romping |
| films | manager | merry | fad | characters |

1. At first, Disney's idea was _____.

☐ _ _ _ _

2. Mickey's voice was high-_____.

_ _ _ _ _ ☐ _

3. Cartoon _____ should be fun.

_ _ _ _ ☐ _ _ _ _ _

4. Another word for happy is _____.

_ _ _ _ ☐

5. Some thought talking movies were a _____.

☐ _ _

6. Disney talked to the Colony Theater's _____.

_ ☐ _ _ _ _ _

7. Disney drew a _____ little mouse.

_ _ ☐ _ _

8. *The Jazz Singer* _____ in New York City.

☐ _ _ _ _ _

9. Mickey had _____ shoes.

_ _ _ _ _ _ ☐

10. People liked _____ made with sound.

_ _ _ _ ☐

Writing Your Ideas

■ Imagine you met Mickey Mouse. On a separate sheet of paper, write what you think Mickey might say.

Remembering What You Read

■ Answer the questions.

1. Why did Lilly Disney like the name "Mickey Mouse?" _____
_____
_____

2. What was the name of the world's first talking cartoon? _____
_____

3. Who was the voice of Mickey Mouse? _____
_____

4. What did movie fans think of the world's first talking cartoon?
_____
_____
_____

Thinking Critically—Sequence

■ Number the sentences to show the order in which things happened in the story. The fist one is done for you.

_____ *The Jazz Singer* opened in New York City.

_____ Mickey Mouse celebrated 60 years as a cartoon star.

_____ *Steamboat Willie* opened at the Colony Theater.

_____ Walt Disney named his new character "Mickey Mouse."

__1__ Walt Disney made two silent cartoons.

WRONG-WAY RIEGELS

January 1, 1929—Roy Riegels had only one thing on his mind as he ran down the football field in Pasadena, California, today. He wanted to score six points in the Rose Bowl game. Riegels had the ball and was running like the wind. He heard someone chasing him. He also heard the crowd roar. But he did *not* hear fans screaming, "Turn around! Turn around!" Riegels was running the wrong way!

Riegels' Big Break

Roy Riegels was a star on the University of California football team. He was hoping to lead his team to a big Rose Bowl win over Georgia Tech. Over 70,000 people came to watch the action that New Year's Day. Across the country, millions more listened on their radios.

Both teams played strong **defense**. There was still no score in the middle of the second quarter. That was when Roy Riegels got his break. A Georgia Tech player **fumbled** the ball. It bounced across the field. Riegels quickly grabbed it. He began to run the 40 yards to the Georgia Tech **end zone**.

Before he had gone very far, he was hit by a Georgia Tech **lineman**. Riegels spun around, but did not fall. He hung onto the football and managed to break free. Then he took off down the field.

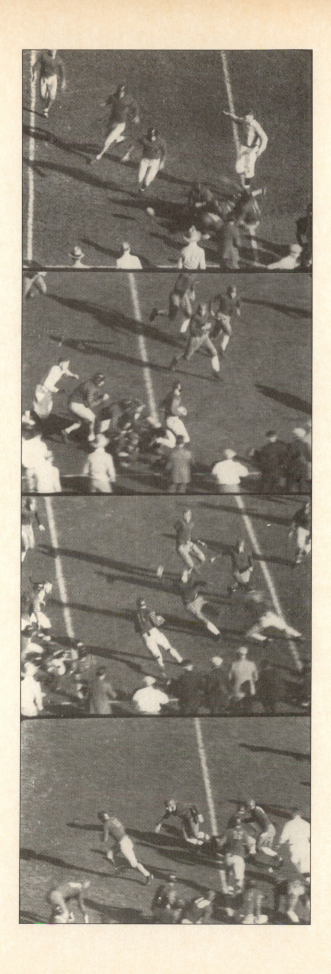

Roy Riegels recovers a fumble, and then he is spun around by a lineman. In the last frame he begins running the wrong way.

83

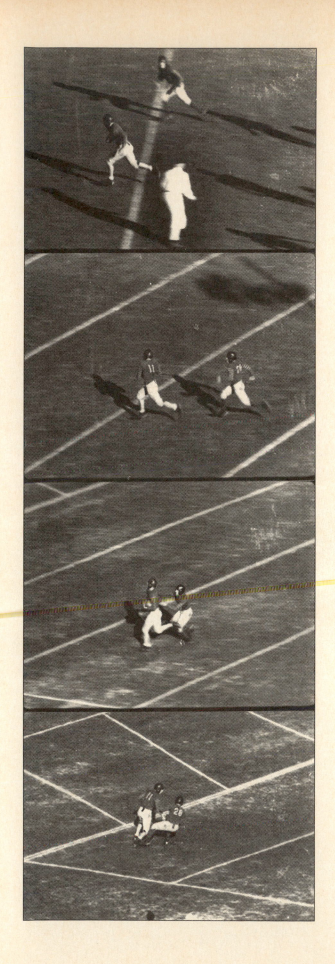

Turn Around! Turn Around!

Riegels did not know it, but the lineman had turned him around. Riegels had lost his sense of direction. He was now headed toward his own end zone!

The crowd could not believe it. Some screamed wildly. Others just stared. The Georgia Tech players were as surprised as the fans. They didn't know what do to. They just stood watching Riegels race the wrong way down the field.

Only one player sprang to action. He was Riegel's **teammate**, Benny Lom. He ran after Riegels. "Turn around! Turn around!" he cried. But Riegels didn't hear him.

Lom knew that if Riegels made it to the end zone, Georgia Tech would get two points. Lom had to stop him! He thought about trying to **tackle** Riegels. But he didn't dare. A tackle might cause Riegels to drop the ball. Then Georgia Tech would be in great shape to score a touchdown.

Benny Lom runs after Riegels and stops him on their own two yard line.

So Lom ran **frantically** after Riegels. Finally he was able to reach out and grab Riegels' shoulder. "Stop!" he yelled into Riegels' ear. This time Riegels heard him. The two players fell to the ground. They were on their own two yard line.

The Final Score

Now, at last, Riegels saw what he had done. His teammates rushed over to him. They patted him on the back and told him not to feel bad. "Don't worry," one said. "We'll just **punt** the ball."

California did punt. But Georgia Tech **blocked** the kick. The ball rolled out of the California end zone, giving Georgia Tech a two-point **safety**. These two points proved to be very important. Each team went on to score one touchdown, and California made its point after the touchdown. The final score was 8-7 in favor of Georgia Tech. If it hadn't been for "Wrong-Way Riegels," the University of California would have won the 1929 Rose Bowl game.

Riegels after his mistake

Building Vocabulary

■ To complete the sentences choose a word from the box. Write the word on the blanks after the sentence. The letters in the boxes will spell the answer to number 10.

blocked	frantically	end zone	tackle	lineman
safety	defense	fumbled	punt	

1. Lom was not trying to _____ Riegels.

   ☐ _ _ _ _ _

2. Georgia Tech _____ the kick.

   _ _ _ _ _ ☐ _

3. Lom ran _____ after Riegels.

   _ _ _ _ _ ☐ _ _ _ _

4. Riegels was hit by a _____.

   _ _ _ _ ☐ _ _

5. A Georgia Tech player _____ the ball.

   _ _ _ _ ☐ _ _ _

6. A _____ is worth two points.

   _ _ _ _ ☐ _ _

7. California tried to _____ the ball.

   _ _ _ ☐ _ _

8. The ball rolled out of the _____.

   ☐ _ _ _ _ _ _

9. Both teams played strong _____.

   _ _ _ _ _ ☐ _

10. What were Benny Lom and Roy Riegels? _____

Writing Your Ideas

■ Imagine you are Roy Riegels. On a separate sheet of paper, write a journal entry titled "My Worst Day."

Remembering What You Read

■ Some of the statements below are true. Others are false. Place a check in front of the three things that happened in the story.

_____ 1. Roy Riegels tackled Benny Lom.

_____ 2. The University of California beat Georgia Tech.

_____ 3. Roy Riegels played in the 1929 Rose Bowl game.

_____ 4. Benny Lom ran after Roy Riegels.

_____ 5. Roy Riegels ran the wrong way.

Building Skills—Read a Table

■ Use the table to answer the questions.

Rose Bowl Results 1928-1932			
Year	_Winner_	_Loser_	_Score_
1928	Stanford	Pittsburgh	7-6
1929	Georgia Tech	California	8-7
1930	Southern California	Pittsburgh	47-14
1931	Alabama	Washington State	24-0
1932	Southern California	Tulane	21-12

1. What team won the most Rose Bowls during these years? _____

_____

2. What team lost twice during these years? _____

3. In what year did the winner score the most points? _____

4. Who won the Rose Bowl in 1931? _____

Glossary

accommodate, page 63
To accommodate someone means to go out of your way to meet his or her needs.

advancing, page 11
To advance means to move forward.

advice, page 15
Advice is an idea that someone gives you to help you answer a question or solve a problem.

amendment, page 11
An amendment is a change made to a law.

anarchists, page 28
Anarchists are people who believe that all governments are bad.

ancient, page 41
Ancient means from times long past.

anniversary, page 70
An anniversary is the day of the year when something important once happened. Their wedding anniversary is on May 20.

approved, page 12
To approve something means to agree to it.

archeologists, page 42
Archeologists study the way people lived long ago. They get information by digging up bits of old cities and towns.

arrested, page 28
To be arrested means to be caught and put in jail by the police.

assistants, page 73
Assistants are people who help someone do something.

background, page 49
The background is what is behind something else. Staying in the background means not attracting attention to oneself.

banned, page 23
If you are banned from doing something, you are not allowed to do it.

bargain, page 65
To bargain means to try to work out the terms of a deal.

blocked, page 85
To block means to knock down a ball that has been kicked or thrown.

brilliant, page 45
Brilliant means very bright.

brushed up, page 36
If you brushed up on something you practiced it.

called, page 57
To call means to ask someone to come. We called the ambulance when we saw the wreck.

canning, page 51

To can means to put food into a jar or can in order to store it for a long time.

career, page 50

A person's career is the work that he or she does in life. She chose nursing as her career.

characters, page 77

A character is a person in a movie, book, or other story.

charges, page 50

Charges are statements saying that a person has done something against the law.

coffin, page 41

A coffin is a box in which a dead body is placed before it is buried.

committee, page 31

A committee is a people who work together to do a certain job.

Congress, page 11

Congress is the group of government leaders who make the laws.

contract, page 65

A contract is a written agreement.

Creationist, page 56

A Creationist is a person who believes the Bible story of how the world was made. Creationists do not believe in evolution.

customs, page 35

Customs are ways of doing things that are shared by a large group of people.

Darwinists, page 55

Darwinists are people who believe Charles Darwin's idea of evolution.

decent, page 23

Decent means proper and good.

defend, page 56

To defend someone is to act in a way to protect that person. A lawyer defends someone by trying to show that the person is not guilty.

defense, page 83

Defense means trying to keep the other team from scoring points.

deliberately, page 19

Something that is done deliberately is done on purpose.

demanded, page 5

To demand means to ask or insist for something in a strong way.

demands, page 65

Demands are statements of what you feel you must get.

denied, page 11

To deny means to refuse to give something to someone.

deserved, page 64

To deserve something means to be worthy of it.

device, page 69

A device is an object or machine made for a certain use.

devoted, page 64

To devote yourself to something means to give your time and attention to that thing.

directors, page 36

A director is the person who guides the actors in a movie.

end zone, page 83

The end zones are at each end of the football field.

enormous, page 77

Enormous means very big.

errors, page 21

An error is a mistake. In baseball, an error is when one of the players makes a poor play.

evolution, page 55

Evolution is the idea that all living things developed over millions of years from simpler forms of life.

executed, page 31

To be executed is to be put to death.

existed, page 43

To exist means to be real. It is sometimes hard to believe dinosaurs ever existed.

experts, page 57

Experts are people who know a lot about a subject.

extra, page 36

An extra is an actor who plays a small part in a movie.

fad, page 78

A fad is something that is well liked for a short time. That haircut was a fad last year.

films, page 77

A film is a movie.

fined, page 59

If you are fined you have to pay money as punishment for something wrong you did. He was fined fifty dollars for speeding.

fixed, page 19

To fix something means to arrange for it to come out a certain way.

fled, page 35

Fled means ran away.

former, page 64

Former means in the past. A former job is a job you used to have.

frantically, page 85

Frantically means wildly and with great fear.

fumbled, page 83

To fumble the ball means to drop it.

future, page 35

Future means the time that is yet to come.

grand jury, page 22

A grand jury is a group of people who decide if a person will be charged with a crime.

grateful, page 36

Grateful means thankful.

grim, page 63

Something that is grim is difficult and offers little hope that it will get better.

guilty, page 22

To be guilty is to have done something wrong or against the law.

impeached, page 50

To impeach is to accuse a person holding office of acting in a wrong way. If the person is found guilty he or she is removed from office.

initials, page 51

An initial is the first letter of a name. The initials for Maria Rios are "M.R."

innocent, page 28

Innocent means not guilty.

invented, page 69

To invent means to make something that no one has ever made before.

involved, page 12

To be involved in something means to be part of it.

items, page 45

Items are things. I have three items I need to buy at the drug store.

jury, page 29

A jury is a group of people who decide whether a person is guilty of a crime.

justice, page 5

Justice means fairness for everyone.

kidnap, page 37

To kidnap means to capture and hold someone by force.

land, page 21

To land something means to get it. To land the goods on someone means to prove he or she has done something wrong.

lineman, page 83

A lineman is a football player who tries to keep the other team from getting to the player with the ball.

lungs, page 71

Lungs are the part of the body used for breathing.

manager, page 79

A manager is a person who runs a store or other business.

merry, page 77

Merry means happy.

mistreatment, page 5

Mistreatment means bad or cruel treatment.

movement, page 6

A movement is a group of people who join together to work for something they think is important.

nickname, page 51

A nickname is a name that people use instead of using the person's real name.

on call, page 63

If you are on call, you must be ready to go to work whenever you are needed. The doctor was on call every third night.

opened, page 78

To open means to begin. The opening of a movie is the day when it is first shown to people.

order, page 55

An order is a group of plants or animals that share certain features.

organized, page 21

Something that is set up in an orderly way. Baseball is an organized sport.

pennant, page 19

A pennant is a flag given to the baseball team that finishes first in its league.

persuasive, page 6

If you are persuasive, you are able to get people to agree with you.

pioneer, page 73

A pioneer is someone who leads the way to a new place or a new idea.

pitched, page 79

Pitch is how high or low a sound is.

politics, page 5

Politics is the study of government and power. Politics are also a person's opinions about government.

powerful, page 49

Powerful means strong and important.

pressed, page 59

To press someone means to push him or her to do something. Her father pressed her to tell the truth.

public, page 50

Public means having to do with government.

punt, page 85

To punt, a football player drops the ball and kicks it to the other team.

rejected, page 7

To be rejected means to be turned away.

research, page 73

Research is a careful study done to gather information.

respect, page 64

Respect is the honor you show someone when you think highly of him or her.

role, page 37

A role is the part that an actor plays. Rachel had the role of the queen in the school play.

romping, page 77

Romping means to play in a loud, happy way.

safety, page 85

To score a safety a player knocks down the ball behind his own goal line.

sealed, page 41

Sealed means closed tightly.

sex, page 11

Sex means one of two groups—male or female.

Keeping Score

1. Count the number of correct answers you have for each activity.
2. Write these numbers in the boxes in the chart.
3. Ask your teacher to give you a score (maximum score 5) for Writing Your Ideas.
4. Add up the numbers to get a final score.

Stories	Building Vocabulary	Writing Your Ideas	Remembering What You Read	Building Skills	Thinking Critically	Score
Marcus Garvey Calls for African Nation						/24
Women Get the Vote!						/22
Say It Ain't So, Joe!						/26
Guilty or Not Guilty?						/21
Novarro a Star						/23
King Tut's Tomb Found!						/23
He's Out, But She's In!						/25
"Monkey Trial" Begins Today!						/21
Sleeping Car Porters Unite						/20
First Rocket Fired!						/23
World's First Talking Cartoon						/24
Wrong-Way Riegels						/22

Answer Key

Marcus Garvey Calls for African Nation   Pages 4–9

Building Vocabulary
    Part A: 1-c, 2-c, 3-a, 4-b, 5-a, 6-a
    Part B: 1. politics, 2. mistreatment,
                3. Universal, 4. united

Writing Your Ideas Answers will vary.

Remembering What You Read
1. The purpose was to draw all black people together.
2. It was a newspaper Marcus Garvey started.
3. It went broke.
4. He hoped to start it in Liberia.

Thinking Critically—Drawing Conclusions
1. he had to go to work.
2. whites controlled the country.
3. he wanted blacks to support the UNIA themselves.
4. he was not a good business manager.
5. he was a great black leader who came from that country.

Women Get The Vote!   Pages 10–17

Building Vocabulary
Across: 1. advancing, 3. amendment, 5. squared off, 6. sex, 7. involved, 8. advice, 9. denied
Down: 2. Congress, 3. approved, 4. suffrage

Writing Your Ideas Answers will vary.

Remembering What You Read
1-c, 2-b, 3-c, 4-a

Building Skills—Use a Table
1. Illinois
2. New York and Illinois
3. 46 women

Say It Ain't So, Joe   pages 18–25

Building Vocabulary 1-h, 2-c, 3-i, 4-j, 5-f, 6-d, 7-g, 8-e, 9-b, 10-a

Writing Your Ideas Answers will vary.

Remembering What You Read 2, 3, 4

Thinking Critically—Fact or Opinion
1-o, 2-f, 3-f, 4-o, 5-o, 6-o, 7-f, 8-f,

Guilty or Not Guilty?   Pages 26–33

Building Vocabulary
    Part A: 1. arrested, 2. anarchists, 3. jury,
                4. Committee
    Part B: 1-a, 2-b, 3-b, 4-a, 5-a, 6-b

Writing Your Ideas Answers will vary.

Remembering What You Read
1-c, 2-c, 3-b, 4-a

Building Skills—Use a Diagram
1. An arrested person faces a grand jury first in a criminal trial.
2. If a person is found guilty, punishment begins after the trial.
3. A grand jury decides if an arrested person should be brought to trial.
4. If the person is found guilty, then punishment begins.

Novarro a Star   Pages 34–39

Building Vocabulary
Across: 6. directors, 7. extra, 8. future, 9. sly, 10. fled
Down: 1. kidnap, 2. role, 3. customs, 4. grateful, 5. brushed up

Writing Your Ideas Answers will vary.

Remembering What You Read 2, 4, 5

Thinking Critically—Cause and Effect
1. they no longer felt safe there.
2. his father became ill.
3. she saw how good he was.
4. he wanted to be an actor.
5. it sounded handsome and was easy to remember.

King Tut's Tomb Found!   Pages 40–47

Building Vocabulary
1. valuables, 2. sponsor, 3. existed, 4. sealed, 5. archeologists, 6. items, 7. ancient, 8. coffin, 9. tomb, 10. CODE WORD: BRILLIANT

Writing Your Ideas Answers will vary.

Remembering What You Read
1. He was an ancient Egyptian king.
2. He paid for Carter's digging for 15 years.

3. Thieves had destroyed them.
4. He saw gold objects everywhere.

Building Skills—Use a Map
1. Valley of the Kings, Badari, and Beni Hasan
2. Red Sea and Mediterranean Sea
3. south
4. Alexandria

He's Out, But She's In!   Pages 48–53

Building Vocabulary
1-c, 2-h, 3-i, 4-f, 5-j, 6-g, 7-b, 8-e, 9-a, 10-d

Writing Your Ideas Answers will vary.

Remembering What You Read 1-a, 2-b, 3-c, 4-c, 5-a

Thinking Critically—Sequence 2, 5, 3, 1, 4

"Monkey Trial" Begins Today!   Pages 54–61

Building Vocabulary
Across: 1. called, 4. turned, 7. fined, 8. evolution, 9. order, 10. Creationist
Down: 2. Darwinists, 3. pressed, 5. experts, 6. defend

Writing Your Ideas Answers will vary.

Remembering What You Read
1. He taught evolution which was against the law in Tennessee.
2. His lawyer was Clarence Darrow.
3. He thought the whole idea of evolution was wrong.
4. Bryan became confused.

Building Skills—Read a Graph
1. the United States
2. Protestant religion
3. 4%
4. Protestant, Catholic, and Jewish religions

Sleeping Car Porters Unite   Pages 62–67

Building Vocabulary
Part A: 1-d, 2-c, 3-g, 4-a, 5-b, 6-f, 7-e
Part B: 1-a, 2-b, 3-b

Writing Your Ideas Answers will vary.

Remembering What You Read
1, 2, 5

Thinking Critically—Main Ideas
2, 4

First Rocket Fired!   Pages 68–75

Building Vocabulary
Part A: 1. pioneer, 2. research, 3. spacecraft
Part B: 1-e, 2-a, 3-f, 4-g, 5-b, 6-c, 7-d

Writing Your Ideas Answers will vary.

Remembering What You Read
1-b, 2-c, 3-a, 4-a

Building Skills—Use a Time Line
1. He climbed the tree in 1899.
2. No.
3. 1913
4. 1882

World's First Talking Cartoon   Pages 76–81

Building Vocabulary
1. vague, 2. pitched, 3. characters, 4. merry, 5. fad, 6. manager, 7. romping, 8. opened, 9. enormous, 10. films
CODE WORDS: VERY FAMOUS

Writing Your Ideas Answers will vary.

Remembering What You Read
1. It was short and friendly.
2. *Steamboat Willie*
3. Walt Disney
4. They loved it.

Thinking Critically—Sequence 3, 5, 4, 2, 1

Wrong Way Riegels   Pages 82–87

Building Vocabulary
1. tackle, 2. blocked, 3. frantically, 4. lineman, 5. fumbled, 6. safety, 7. punt, 8. end zone, 9. defense, 10. CODE WORD: TEAMMATES

Writing Your Ideas Answers will vary.

Remembering What You Read 3, 4, 5

Building Skills—Read a Table
1. Southern California
2. Pittsburgh
3. 1930
4. Alabama